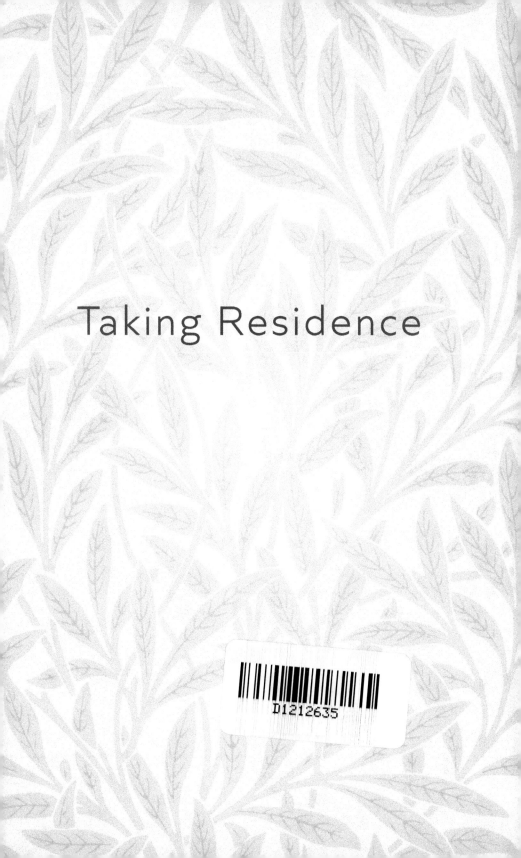

Taking Residence

Taking Residence

poems by

Wally Swist

SHANTI ARTS PUBLISHING
BRUNSWICK, MAINE

Taking Residence

Published by Shanti Arts Publishing
Interior and cover design by Shanti Arts Designs

Cover image: iStock.com/mysondanube

Source: *Tree of Song: Poems by Federico Garcia Lorca*, Translated from
the Spanish by Alan Brilliant, Greensboro, SC: Unicorn Press, 1973;
*Flame of Love: Poems of the Spanish Mystics: San Juan de La Cruz (St.
John of the Cross}, Santa Teresa De Jesus (St. Teresa of Avila)*, English
Translation by Loren G. Smith, Staten Island, NY: Alba House/Society
of Saint Paul, 2005; *Selected Poems: Giuseppe Ungaretti*, Translated
by Andrew Frisardi, New York, NY: Farrar, Straus and Giroux, 2004.

Shanti Arts LLC
193 Hillside Road
Brunswick, Maine 04011

shantiarts.com

Printed in the United States of America

ISBN: 978-1-951651-84-8 (softcover)

Library of Congress Control Number: 2021938082

for the readers of these poems

and

for Tevis Kimball

That prayer has great power which a person makes with all his might. It makes a sour heart sweet, a sad heart merry, a poor heart rich, a foolish heart wise, a timid heart brave, a sick heart well, a blind heart full of sight, a cold heart ardent. It draws down the great God into the little heart; it drives the hungry soul up into the fullness of God; it brings together two lovers, God and the soul, in a wonderous place where they speak of much love.

—Mechthild of Magdeburg

And what rule do you think I walked by? Truly a strange one, but the best in the whole world. I was guided by an implicit faith in God's goodness, and therefore led to the study of the most obvious and common things. For thus I thought within myself: God being, as generally believed, infinite in goodness, it is most consonant and agreeable with His nature that the best things be most common.

—Thomas Traherne

CONTENTS

HOVERING MOON

MNEMOSYNE: A SUITE FOR THE MUSES

SIXTEEN TRANSLATIONS FROM THE ITALIAN OF GIUSEPPE UNGARETTI

SHARING STORIES AT LUNCH

ACKNOWLEDGMENTS

The author is grateful to the editors of the following publications in which these poems originally appeared, often in an earlier version.

All Roads Will Lead You Home: "Shades of Green"

The Ashvamegh International Journal & Literary Magazine (India): "Sundarbans" and "The White Stag"

Buddhist Poetry Review: "Aridity and the Spiritual Life," "Green Heron, First Day of Autumn," "Lingering beside Long Pond, Indian Summer," "Mirage," "The Order of Things," and "Red-bellied Woodpecker"

Common Ground Review: "Kingdom of Heaven"

The Deronda Review (Israel): "Gambol" and "Interstice"

Empirical Magazine: "Mink""

Eureka Street (Australia): "Giraffes," "Hitleresque," and "To the Time Remaining"

Ezra: An Online Journal of Translation: "Canto/Song" and "Grido/Outburst"

The Galway Review (Ireland): "Always" and "Taking Residence"

Many Hands: A Magazine for Holistic Health: "Hummingbird and Star," "The Snake" and "Windhorse"

Noctua Review: "Rock and Meadow"

Peacock Journal: "A Dream like Ours"

Pensive: A Global Journal of Spirituality and the Arts: "A Conversation"

Poetry East: "Euterpe Singing"

Puckerbrush Review: "The Fire," "The Inspired Life," "The Mole" and "What Is Familiar"

The RavensPerch: Adding Breadth to Words: "Cancion Del Mariquita/Song of the Ladybug," "La Luna Asoma/Hovering Moon" and "Suma de perfección/Sum of Perfection"

Sahara: A Journal of New England Poetry: "Mnemosyne," "Rituals" and "Wabi and Sabi"

Still Point Arts Quarterly: "Glass"

The Woven Tale Press: "Adelina de Paseo/Song of Adeline, the Streetwalker," "Arbol de Cancion/Tree of Song" and "Balanza/Balance"

"Accompaniment" was issued as a limited edition letterpress broadside by Adastra Press.

"A Conversation" also appeared in *Eureka Street* (Australia).

"Dream of Judita Vaiciunaite" was translated into Lithuanian by Kornelijus Platelis and appeared in Literatura ir Menas (Vilnius, Lithuania).

Some of the poems appearing in "Part Three: Modern Bestiary" previously appeared in an earlier version in *The View of the River* (Kelsay Books/Aldrich Press, 2017). "Aridity and the Spiritual Life" initially appeared as two separate poems, both in earlier versions, individually entitled "Aridity" and "The Spiritual Life."

The eleven poems comprising "Part Five: Mnemosyne: A Suite for the Muses" initially appeared as individual poems, in earlier versions, and not in sequence in *Huang Po and the Dimensions of Love* (Southern Illinois University Press, 2012) and *Invocation* (Lamar University Press, 2015).

"Sharing Stories at Lunch" was published as a poem-in-a-pamphlet in a limited edition letterpress edition by master printer Clarence Wolfshohl at his El Grito de Lobo Press in Fulton, Missouri, in the spring of 2021.

Part One

TAKING RESIDENCE

ROCK AND MEADOW

I enjoyed hearing the anecdote
of her child-self, at eight, when she perched

on the rock that she claimed as a throne
in the meadow near her home,

ruling over her peers in the neighborhood with
her scepter, or rather a part of a deadfall stick.

Now, how wonderful is that? I will never forget it.
How true it is that whole mystical tableau

has transcended itself, in many ways in her life,
and has morphed into the corner office

she now inhabits and works out of, not to mention
so many other forms of her meadow rock

and her eight-year-old child-self.
I can only wish I could stop imagining we were

realized in such a way in our lives: for me to be
that rock for her and for her to be that meadow,

in which she rests upon her throne and watches
the wind's scepter wave over the summer grasses.

TAKING RESIDENCE

Not wanting it to sing too loudly, or for it to fly away,
is learning what it is that is taking residence in the heart.

Not desiring to hold onto it, not wanting for it to dissipate,
is how the presence in the heart requests to be honored—

the visitor making itself known by the murmurs of
its rustling. It is what propels the fountain of it in keeping

its arcing waters from ebbing, only if by resisting what
the heart yearns for, even slightly, which is why the heart

leaps amid all of its windy fluttering. Your loveliness is
as sinuous as the colloquy of birdsong on a summer morning.

ALWAYS

What we will have always
is the vision of our being bathed
in roseate and gold light,

in a reverential beauty,
in a celestial radiance,
in which I hold you always.

What we are now is that we are
changed forever since the light
enabled you to transport

your radiance for me to see
your seraphic form appear
above the divine white light

of your face, for me to be
filled with you always, for us
to be bathed is an awakening

that for us will be with us
always, a breakthrough
in which we see everything anew;

in which the spiritual power
of the awakening emanates
within us, through which

we can feel our connectedness
even over distances,
between us, always.

May we glow with each other
always, as I experience your
presence in waves, your

incandescence, always, brimming
within me, then brimming
again, always. Ask me

whatever you ask of me,
but always know when you ask me
whatever you ask me,

whenever and wherever, know
we are now one, that my answer
will be *yes*, and *yes*, again, always.

A CONVERSATION

He says, "Think of your awakening
as the event that it is, that it perpetuates,
that its ascendency is as resilient as
a tungsten filament radiating with you."

She says, "Tell me more." He says,
"When I drive to the studio in
the morning, I experience independent
moments of my life but am aware

that they are all interconnected—
as we are all enmeshed, as in
the metaphor for interbeing,
the jeweled net of Indra." She says,

"Yes, we're all one, but tell me more."
"By the time I drive through
those s-curves by Gagne's Store before
the Granby Road, and look out at

that *plein* of uncut meadow
on the other side of the street, I see
that I am present in the moment
when I was five, wearing a captain's

hat, gazing over the ocean from
the shore, on a school field trip,
by a lighthouse, on a clear day,
near Miami; or am one with you

the day we hiked the Notch that
brilliant October day when we
cavorted among the colored leaves,
the sunlight flooding through

the partially defoliated trees."
She asks, "Is there more?" He says,
"Yes, there is always more, every
changing moment is eternal, that

is what is our eternity truly is,
and there are as many awakenings
as there are stars in the sky,
and to experience that is to observe

that tungsten glow inside you,
to feel its filament radiating
within, and to feel your life unfurl,
in your ascendency, as does

a scarf rippling in the wind—
all of it interconnected, each sequin
reflecting the other, as in Indra's
bejeweled net, all of it aglow."

THE WEIGHT OF THE WOOD

To see the sheared
    maple branch lying
        on the ground in the rain

was an astonishment
    but to begin to lift
        the weight of the wood

after the storm was
    a palpable lesson
        in humility, of coming

to terms with the extent
    of one's strength in
        moving what was not just

massive but was heavy
    in sheer girth and length.
        What offered continued

pause was first axing
    the smaller limbs, then
        using a sharpened saw

to cut through the smaller
    trunks bifurcating out
        from the main one, sawdust

accumulating along with
    my sweat dampening
        the grass in ninety degree

heat, all the while hearing
    a chainsaw buzzing in
        a neighbor's yard several

houses away, which
    automatically began
        pushing the groove even

further in just being
      grateful for having a hand
            tool and the strength

in the grasp of hands
      and in the use of my own
            agile limbs, to break

the maple down,
      so I could move it
            in one smaller piece

after another. But it was
      certainly the veritable
            feel of the weight of

the wood itself
      that gave the day its
            dimension and heft,

and the ensuing
      satisfaction in even such
            exhaustion afterwards

in straining to move
      what resists movement,
            to transcend limitations;

while still finding
      myself amid what
            was, until only recently,

the dynamism of wild
      branches swaying on
            every wind and rocking

in any breeze under
      the interminable constancy
            of an ever-changing sky.

INTERSTICE

It is Friday and I am finishing
for the week in the studio,
but I pause between projects

to reheat some coffee. It is late
morning. The sky is overcast
but the day is still cool. August

lushness making branches
hang languorously, still weeks
from the harvest and autumn

chill. Although I have begun to
dodder some, and allow myself
to feel that I am slowing down

even though I am not quite seventy,
I think about Art Beck relaying
how Willis Barnstone, at ninety,

living in Paris, is still writing four
sonnets per day. Sometimes just
standing between one point and

another needs to be just enough—
that still place between doing
and not doing, since immanence

and distance clarifies into
the perceived present, of being
alive in this one moment

for all time, dew still on the grass.

MS. HART

was known as Miss Hart
since the honorific then specified her
being unmarried and denotes
a time before feminist ethics prevailed,

although the appellation only inferred
that Ms. Hart, especially at her age,
was a spinster, and one who also lived
with her mother. She was my music

teacher in grammar school, and always
gave me an A. I remember her
blowing into her pitch pipe to find
the correct key, and her leading

the class in chorale. She was robust
in her performance and accentuated
her presentation of each song.
She sang *Sweetly Sings the Donkey,*

and I can still hear her cantering voice
rise in leading the chorus. She choose
me to mow her lawn, since I gained
a reputation for mowing neighborhood

lawns, and when I finished mowing
she would invite me into her home
so she could pay me. Her garage
and basement floors were impeccably

clean and they were freshly painted.
Her living room shone with a ring
of crystal in the sunlight,
and her aged mother would always

sit in an arm chair, and politely chat
with me, one time listening to
my question about the photograph
in a silver frame of the handsome

naval officer atop the television,
but emerging out of the hallway
with my payment for having mown
the lawn was Ms. Hart, who answered

in a whisper, that he had been
her fiancé during the second world war,
and that his aircraft carrier had
gone down with all hands on-board,

and I will never forget, even in
the radiance of the lit room,
the irrefutable penumbra of darkness
that spread beneath that photograph,

which seemed to portray
the weight of the evident sadness
that lingered to limn the wrinkles
beneath her doleful eyes.

HITLERESQUE

Zeig Heil,
Herr Donald, *Zeig Heil.*
Autocrat,
Zeitgeist dictator,
wolfish ghoul,
you frighten us

with your rage, your terror,
your glinting white teeth
flecked with spittle
throughout your ranting stump speeches,
Herr Donald,
Herr Trump.

Even in the hard rain
of October,
puddled with burnished
colors of fallen leaves,
your name echoes
in the hallowed darkness,

ricochets around
the abyss you inhabit
with the evil you have created,
Zeig Heil,
Herr Donald, Herr Trump.
Little Putin with small hands,

monster whose monstrous
actions double down on each other;
hater, liar, predator, scoundrel, cheat,
if we could we would unveil you,
disaster of disasters,
and expose you for whom and what you are,
and make an example

of your narcissistic reviled glory
for what it is
and flush you into
a deep state black hole—
a conspiracy theory
of your own making

from which you won't be able
to escape—
so we could be remade
without your psycho power grabbing
and sociopathological
obstreperous outlandishness

mocking whatever is worthy and fine,
sowing vicissitudes of despair.
Zeig Heil,
Herr Donald, *Zeig Heil,*
may your obdurate soul
blacken in hell's gravity,

for your crimes against humanity,
may those flames burn you
in the same way you have
intentionally scorched the earth
with your bizarre displays of idiocy
and your whipping up

the recklessly wild lunacy
that has brought down goodness and decency
and has dragged that
through the streets
where your unhinged rhetoric,
try as it may,

will never be potent enough
to spoil our sunniest of mornings,
since it is we
who will topple you
by our standing firm
in opposing your wretchedness and wrath.

DAILY PRACTICE

1. Inner Prayer

I have practiced the 'Jesus Prayer,'
for the last half century, since I was twenty. I often use it
as my mantra, to pray for others, as did the pilgrim

on his journey, which he documented in his book,
The Way of the Pilgrim. I, similarly, practice kinhin—
walking meditation, which arises from my Buddhist studies.

2. Passage Meditation and Daily Review

My spiritual practice is also augmented by daily
passage meditation from Eknath Easwaran's *Words to Live By.*
This practice is furthered with another reverent

meditation on a prayer card from Father Ralph DiOrio, a non-
denominational healing priest, which is
simply entitled, "Sacred Heart of Jesus, I place my trust in you."

I close out my daily spiritual practice
with a daily review, as I have learned in my years of
deep reading of *The Guide Lectures,* channeled by Eva Pierrakos.

3. Tonglen

A breathing exercise: first, on the in-breath, breathing the pain
of others in, and then on the out-breath, breathing their pain out—
for blessing, for the purposes of healing

those who are being attended to, say, by a passing ambulance.
You can even become an adept of this while standing
in line at a checkout at the grocery store. Pema Chödrön describes

this ancient Buddhist practice
as taking and sending: with each in-breath, we take away
someone's pain; then with each out-breath, we send them relief.

WHAT IS LEFT

of you, whether long or short,
hovers as does a mirage
in the distance

and *distance* is
the medium in which
you conceal your secrets
about what and how much

time that remains but it is
up to us as to what
to do with whatever amount
of the measure

of our lives we have
yet to use, which then
provides us with
the exigency towards

momentum in
propelling our aspirations,
our positive intentions,
the proactive propulsion

of our ascendant arc,
and if not our own
then whatever it is
we can do for others,

or at least another
other than ourselves
in either an instant
or in a meaningful

hour, the most fervid
day, which might cast
itself as a prototype for
another that may
lay the karmic riprap

for more after that as long
as our purposes remain
resolute, as may our

time remaining, which then
portends that whatever
the amount we strive
to appreciate and savor

the instant of our lives,
which perpetuates beyond
the timelessness,
in which you only dress

yourself in appearances,
since whatever remains
beyond you is sustained
by the impediment of

your inherent calculation
whose restrictions only
limit what is bound by you,
since however much

you are and whatever
the time you are remaining
to whomever and forever
long lasts without lasting.

Part Two

THE ORDER OF THINGS

THE ORDER OF THINGS

in memory of Robert Winne

1.

One pink-red rose among rosettes
Blooms beside the flickering prismatic
Spider webs strung among the florescence
Of yarrow and mint leaves,
Where we stood last autumn
When you were still alive,
This brilliant June morning; birdsong rising
From the sheen of the needles of hemlock
Branches along the path.

2.

Purple flags of wild iris
And the large yellow buttons of the corollas
Of oxeye daisies thrive among foxtail grass
Amid the ahness of a single flower head
Of orange hawkweed; one whole shoulder
Of the trail up to the Peace Pagoda
Bursting white with mountain laurel;
Some of their flower clusters
Shattered after the heavy June rains
And scattered beneath their shrubbery
In the detritus of leaves and dried mud.

3.

The sound of a woodpecker
Rapping on a tree trunk, then stopping,
And rapping again, echoes from afar,
Deeper in the woods. An entire plywood
Platform of stone sculptures near the crest
Of the last hill are still largely intact, most
Of which have survived the wind and the rain,
Since the last time we walked here.

4.

When I reach the top of the trail
To the open field before the Peace Pagoda,
A mourning cloak circles me several times;
Frogs croak from the Koi pond; a whir
Of electric hand tools buzzes
From workers in the meditation hall,
That much closer to being fully constructed;
The stone lion dooryard guardians,
That we saw being erected on their brick
Dais and plinth, now perennially welcome
The sangha who enter in all of their Shambhala
Strength; images of Avalokiteśvara adorn
Either side of the carved wooden temple
Doors; someone has moved the bench
We would sit on into the small meadow
And placed it farther into the shade.

5.

Pink mountain laurel compliments the color
Of the pond lilies just opening across the water.
Yellow iris blooms among purple clover,
Vetch, and ragged robin.
Fallen white peonies and desiccated rugosa roses
Lay collapsed in the grass or rock in the breeze
That ripples the lines of multi-colored
Prayer flags over the pond
Where the diphthong of one frog answers
The elasticity in the voice of another.

6.

The redness of a Japanese maple shades
The entrance beside a boulder
To the path encircling the pond, but
Does not cover the space left by your absence.
Bumblebees pollinate a stand of phlox,
Their chartreuse petals exclamatory among
The small green fronds of meadow grass;
The diaphanous wings of mating dragonflies,
When they collide, sizzle
Against each other, instantaneously.

7.

When I look deeply into the yellow center
Of the open white pond lily,
It is as if I gaze directly into myself.
Gray-black tadpoles and orange Koi
Skitter through the pond water
When my shadow moves along the shore;
A water snake slithers across
The pond's surface, its head disappearing
Among the cattails and reeds before
The exaggerated cursives of its body.

8.

The first prayer flag on one of the lines
Snaps in a gust, well before the others.
A grouse drums in the birch woods.
A tiger swallowtail flies up and out
Of the petaled shade of the dogwood's
Custard-colored blossoms,
Just beyond the reclining Buddha
In the north niche, the one that
Is said to be entering Parinirvana.

9.

After I circumnavigate the Peace Pagoda,
I find there is nowhere to go,
And that you are one now
With the nothingness that is your home
And will be ours.
Birch leaves rustle in the slightest breeze.
Sunlit patches of stellaria brighten in the grass.
All of this has not happened quite this way
Before; all of this, despite its recurrence,
Will not ever be this way again.

Part Three

MODERN BESTIARY

DREAM OF JUDITA VAICIUNAITE

for Jonas Zdanys

In the dream, she arranges to meet me aboard the cutter.
Our hair streams in the wind, and I ask her about the women

Sitting upon the rocks of the harbor, and standing among
The stony cliffs along the shore, all singing in the polyphony

Of Hildegaard von Bingen, and she informs me that
They protect the city, that they turn away the ships of enemies

And guide the vessels of its friends. Then I ask her about
The ranks of men harvesting the ripe coastal grass for haying,

And she answers me that this is one example how husbandry
Is inculcated into the society, that in another life

Many of the men seen harvesting were proponents
Of selfish means, who favored plundering the earth for profit

Instead of managing the balance of her natural ways.
Aboard the cutter in the dream with the wind in our hair,

She speaks a poem about wreathing a rainbow in the sky
On the day before she died, after a night of heavy rain,

In the book that glows with the images of her beloved Vilnius,
After I turn out the light on the night table, her poems page

Through my mind with the icons of their images of wild
Chamomile, plum blossoms, and bitterns contained

In the lyrics. Dandelion honey, the red of the autumn sage,
The mother-of-pearl clouds about to vanish from the sky

Like the great wings of the sea eagle, who is no longer lonely;
And as dusk is extinguished on its wings, her white hair

Changes again into the black hair of her youth, as I awaken
From the dream with the sound of the cutter still in my ears.

SUNDARBANS

Where four rivers
empty into a confluence of freshwater
forests of mangrove swamps:
Bramaputra, Ganges, Meghna, Padma.

Where four rivers resonate with
a chatter of macaques, and the blade of
the sawfish gleams; where you can hear
the splash of the saltwater crocodile.

Where four rivers
provide sustenance for itinerant fisher-
man and honeygatherers
who range deep into the Sundari groves.

Where four rivers
offer sanctuary for the Bengal tiger, who
is a formidable swimmer, to roam
the Sundarbans of Bangladesh and India.

Where four rivers gather,
fisherman have fashioned masks to wear
on the back of their head to try to thwart
fierce attacks by the Bengal tiger.

Where four rivers flow
it is said that a fisherman fought off such
an attack by using his fishing pole
in his defense of a tiger's teeth and claws.

Where four rivers stream
together in a rush, a fisherman on a bank
hears a crackle of sticks, and turns to see
what is about to spring upon him is a tiger.

Where four rivers sweep
toward the sea, honeygatherers walk through
the dark forest carrying the combs
of bees amid the Bengal tiger's echoing roar.

Where four rivers meet,
the mangrove forests are named Sundarbans,
which in Bengali means
beautiful forest, flickering in light and shade.

Where four rivers course
through green mangroves, it is said that only
an infirmed Bengal tiger, one who has lost
some teeth, will attack a boat of fishermen.

MINK

Standing beside the brook pool that winter
morning, where I had scattered the ashes

of my yellow Labrador, bright February sun
igniting the snowbanks into glare, the sound

of its nails over the ice crust just beginning
to escalate into a roar, as it adjusted the long

lithe yard of its stunning black furred body
in its attempt to steer down the slope of one

bank, then another; sunlight flickering off
the radiant oil of its coat, as it veered,

appearing to drift uncontrollably, on a line
straight toward me, so quickly, I didn't even

think of sidestepping over to the left
or dodging right, but remember edging

backward towards the flange of the brook's
icy ledges. When it was only a few feet away

from me, it angled to its right, and in one
fluid wildly acrobatic motion, leapt, after

taking several running steps, to grab hold
of the trunk of the hollow sycamore

on the bank. For a moment, it looked at me,
and I stared back, its claws dug into the tree

bark, not with hostility, but as in embracing
the familiarity of its home; before ascending

into the top of the trunk's empty cavern—
the sound of the brook's rush merging with

the sunlight flashing over the frigid water,
clouds of my breath steaming the frosty air.

GAMBOL

The chipmunk is not as ignobly brazen as the squirrel—
not the crazed mad dasher crossing the roadway, then

turning around, with its tail a raised question mark in
the air, always twitching, as the squirrel speeds beneath

the wheels of the moving car. The chipmunk is not as
imprudent or daft as the squirrel, is not at all maniacal, but

behaves more in keeping with an athlete, its white racing
stripes emblazoned on either side of its upper back,

intimating speed, although not in the squirrel's mindlessly
frenzied fashion, but more in the way of a sprinter, with

the finish line of the other side of the road its inevitable
destination, a veritable cross-road dash, acorn in mouth,

its four feet engaged in the very definition of what
the word *bolt* means. However, as much as squirrels

may be fleet they are not known for being friendly, such
impertinent creatures as they are, muttering their harsh

chatter, lunatic interlopers always setting limits that exhibit
a boundless temerity. Whereas, a chipmunk I chanced

upon hiking Mount Lafayette, as I stopped mid-mountain
for a rest, volunteered to join me in a snack of trail mix,

tame enough to eat some right out of my outstretched hand,
filling its mouth at various intervals until the pouches

in its cheeks bulged, and upon surfeit it returned to its hole
dug into the earth beneath white pine, only to emerge again

for more peanuts and raisins with which it could
line its burrow for leaner times, whom native Americans

called the *one who descends trees headlong,* whose
nicknames include steward and housekeeper—

how we gamboled that summer day, *Tamias striatus,*
both of us bartering trust, having befriended one another.

SHADES OF GREEN

It is elegantly furled
    as if it were a broad leaf curled
        into a bright green body with

a tail. Its head is cocked and its
    antennae are splayed, perhaps,
        not so much in consternation

as in consideration of what
    to do next. Its four lime green
        legs attach themselves to storm

window glass, as if it is in
    perpetual mid-leap, inside-
        looking-out of the half-lifted

storm window, that accommodates
    the air conditioner. When I first
        saw it, I thought it was on

the outside of the glass, which it
    may have been, but now it is
        on the inside of the glass, and

if a grasshopper could be said
    to be keening, then that is what
        it is doing. I look out at it from

where it rests on the clear pane,
    the deep green leaves of a maple
        in full view, and beyond that

the sunnier green
    of the open field before
        the windbreak's hedgerow green.

MIRAGE

To take a walk on the meadow path before
I went to work at the bookstore that afternoon

endowed me with a memory that still swings
like an invisible medallion around my neck,

still perplexing me all these years later. The heat
climbing as the sun rose higher in the sky,

the dry burn of it beginning to swelter in
a building humidity beneath banks of low cumulus.

The two-lane meadow path winding onward
in its gritty tire tracks, split by its grassy tufts

of bent stalks of sedge and spike rush, roughed
by tractor undercarriage and sled. As I walked,

I could feel my sweat beading beneath my shirt,
and before I came upon open meadow on the edge

of the woods, I stopped and turned, only
to look up into the upper branches of the white

oaks, swinging their heavy brooms of leaves,
windswept and lush with their whisking music,

shushing the polyphony of cicadas that fills
the house of summer. When my eyes

spotted them, so unnatural, out of order,
among the swaying of the oaks, leading me

to think that the heat had induced a mirage,
a hallucinogenic vision of the flock

of wild turkeys balancing their unwieldy
bodies high in the trees to perch on the limbs.

I can still see them up there, somewhere
above ground and beyond reason, the heat

of the day hammering the air so that the birds
seemed to mirror themselves in a haze—

wild turkeys that had been able to raise
the heaviness of their bodies up on their pygmy

wings and to have flown into the oaks
along the path, their presence alerting me

to having seen something untoward, freakish,
even in their apparent hiding their seeming

unbidden, out of position, the uneasy but sheer
certainty of knowing their being out of place.

THE FOX TOWER

It became what we could measure
    our notion of manhood against
        by the hardscrabble climb up

the metal girders to the wooden
    blockhouse that crowned the top
        through which we entered by

a trapdoor in the floor. The climb
    was harrowing in our needing
        to grip the metal crossbeams

of the girders, to slither our legs
    and have them find a catch with
        our feet, upon which we would

push our bodies up in making
    our way to the lookout above,
        its windows overseeing what

we referred to as the Pine
    Forest to the east, undisturbed
        meadows to the west, and below us

the empty cages of what was
    discerned as an abandoned fur
        farm, the odor of which we were

inundated with upon entering
    the blockhouse, where old
        pelts and odd tools seemed to be

smeared with the oil of
    the furs. We stood on the precipice
        of pubescence and whatever odd

concept we might have had about
    what manhood could be, what our
        raw instinct led us to believe

we needed to design as a challenge,
    or a series of them, in order to
        earn the privilege of entering

into, and earning, the realm of
    adulthood, looking out at a landscape
        we became to know as familiar,

aware that we would need to exceed
    those boundaries, never being able
        to fathom what really transpired

in the blockhouse, other than
    somehow someone had chosen
        to tan the hides there, high among

the cages below; always pausing before
    we descended again, placing our
        shaky legs on the wobbly metal

joists; imagining what other trials
    we would need to face in order to
        become the men we thought we

might morph into, hanging on in the wind,
    attempting to balance ourselves from
        one loose girder to the next, prior

to surviving our daredevil
    descent downward, in anticipation
        of placing our feet on solid ground.

THE SCENT

I came upon the body of a dead raccoon among
The bracken, its grimace frozen beside the ice-sheathed

Brook. The way in which its body lay contorted
On the ice crust caused me to think it may have fallen

From an overhanging branch, as I bent, keeping a safe
Distance. Later, on the walk in front of the house,

I thought it was the house cat, the one who always
Wanted to go out, and once out, wanted back in,

Brushing against my trousers, and looked down,
Only to match gazes with the raccoon who had taken

Refuge in the neighbors' carriage house next door.
It must have smelled the scent of the body

Of the dead raccoon on me, possibly sensing I might
Be one of its larger unmasked brethren; and since

I wasn't sure if it were rabid, I stamped one foot
Twice, to spook it away from its rubbing against me.

I could see from the quizzical look of its eyes
That it was unsure why I was dissuading it from

Continuing its spooning, then it bolted, making its
Way through the space beneath the fence separating

The neighbor's yard from ours, looking behind
At me all the while, the click of its paws echoing

Over the salt-stained asphalt, as it slipped back into
Its own mystery of being, of itself as raccoon,

Returning to the icy darkness of the winter night.
Months later, early one summer morning, I saw it

Flicking its tail, both sentry and thief, perched
Atop a telephone pole, peering down on me.

THE SNAKE

Beauty as sinuousness: more than
a foot long; alternate yellow

and brown stripes running the length
of its body, ending in a pointed

black tail. When I needed to walk
past to go to the barn with

my recycling, it didn't move. I was
close enough to bend down to place

it in my hands. Although I was sure
it wouldn't have enjoyed that, so

I didn't. You would have appreciated
being there with me for that moment:

its head poised about five or six
inches off the ground in a right angle

to its body. It was so comfortable
with me that I even walked past it

again on my way to the mail box
on the road. And there it was, head

held high, body curled in fashionable
loops, that were in keeping with

the ease of my interaction with its
primed electric elegance, its watchful

stillness, the penetrating incisiveness
of the dots of its bulging black eyes.

By the time I was back with my mail,
it was gone.

THE MOLE

Blind visionary, whose eyes
are vestigial, you withdraw

deeper into a privacy
never remote enough.

In spring, after heavy rain, rills
of your tunnels cross

the wet ground in the meadow.
Your feet are shaped like small shovels;

even your nose looks like a tuber.
Finding you dead this morning

in the grass, I know whatever
I feared could happened has

already happened, and the years
of darkness have already begun.

HATRED

It is represented in drawings and paintings
as dark because its essence is odious,
an ominous rankling. It repels everything

and absorbs its own suffering. Its weight
overwhelms those who practice its black arts
but those who indulge themselves in such

aberrant devotions often find a visceral thrill
in sticking a pin through the heart
of the kewpie doll designed as the victim

of their rage. If the transgressions are so dire,
there is even a joy in hurling curse after curse
upon those who trespass against us not only in

life, but also far past the grave, in one life after
another. The sheer force of such an epithet
is shrill but beyond our normal range of hearing.

The Harpies' voices raise themselves in a choir.
"The Black Paintings" of Francisco Goya come
to life. His *Witches' Sabbath* or *Aquelarre* are

animated with their subjects filling the sky on
brooms. Like Goya, we paint our canvases with
the palette of darkness from our accrued spleen

from those who have injured us, and we execute
the viscera, twisting and turning in on itself like
a basin of silverfish, or a tub of snakes, onto

the plaster of our innermost rooms, and when
our intentions are discovered, as a wry smile
discerned in the set of the jaw bones of the skull

of a corpse, the presentation of wrath perpetuating
itself, well past the length of our own lives, is
preserved beyond what lies desiccated after our deaths.

GIRAFFES

As Americans, we have learned to live with
a mountain between us that we look up at every day.

Some live on one side of it and some live on another,
as two herds of giraffes might live on a savannah, dotted

with trees. We might have learned that we can no longer
feed on the leaves at the tops of the crowns, but need

to bend our long necks, which we carry on our small body
and relatively short legs, and we have retrained ourselves

to consume the leaves on the lower limbs. As we are
nibbling leaves on the lower branches, we are still seeking

to feed off desiccated leaves higher up on the limbs.
As we browse trunk to trunk, we think of the other herd

on the other side of the mountain; we have not been able to love,
nor have we found a pathway, both of us only having evolved

to being giraffes, roving the woodlands without ever satiating
our hunger, by galloping first in one direction, then another;

and we have not made much of a difference to anyone,
including ourselves, and despite bowing and lifting

our great necks, the best that we can do is to spend
most of the time avoiding the wild dogs of our best intentions.

THE WHITE STAG

The painted box
    with the white stag bounding through
        autumn swale, descending the ridge

below nearly defoliated birch, maple,
    and oak, augurs the otherwordly
        dimension which informs our daily

lives on this plane, from which
    the Celts believed this animal
        was both a herald and messenger.

Although it is also a sign of taboo,
    as in the transgression of Pwyll,
        Prince of Dyfed, and his hounds,

trespassing King Anwan's hunting
    grounds. Arthurian legend honed
        its reliance on the white stag's

ability to evade capture and that
    when seen the sighting proved
        to be an indication to begin a quest,

also denoting the incipience of the hero's
    journey. Saint Eustace, Christian
        martyr, saw a vision of a crucifix

between the antlers of a white stag
    while hunting in ancient Tivoli,
        which precipitated his perseverance

in his faith, despite a litany of afflictions
    which rivaled the tribulations of Job.
        Even Robert Baden-Powell, founder

of world scouting, lectured about
    the white stag, and didn't espouse
        it being hunted, but taught that it was

a symbol of moving onward, not
       without joy, and was emblematic of
           woodswalking itself. Hungarian myth

relays that the brothers Hunor and
       Magor were visited by a white stag,
           and that it led them to Scythia, where-

upon they founded the Magyar tribe.
       C. S. Lewis anointed a white stag to
           steer the sleigh of Jadis, the white witch,

but was responsible for also leading
       the children out of Narnia, which
           intimates the duality of both good and evil.

How this animal furthermore portends
       compassion, is seen in the tale by Kate
           Seredy, *The White Stag,* in which even

Atilla the Hun, known historically as
       the *Scourge of God,* followed this white
           hart on a mythological journey which

brought his people to a new country
       in which they could settle, live in peace.
           It is also said that anyone who is enough

of an adept hunter to snare the white
       stag is then granted three wishes,
           upon which, at this time, I might open

the lid of this painted wooden box,
       which was given to me so generously
           and graciously as a gift, and prudently

lift my eyes up to meet those
       of the white stag and ask for grace
           to abound in my heart and in my home.

WINDHORSE

Slabs of white marble in stacks.
The pictographs carved in them.

Then this thin tablet. My hands
running across the intaglio of a frieze.

Its smoothness in relief.
The celebration of *Bacchus* in honor

of *Equus*.
Unearthing the actual vision of it

in the archeology of dream.
The going to and the digging through

layers of consciousness, as in layers
of earth.

In the city of *Equestrium*.
That is what I heard. The word spoken

as it was spoken.
Workers and trainers

moving here and there, as in a kind
of bas-relief.

Then someone speaking
to me, instructing me with the urgency

in their stentorian voice.
Although I did not

necessarily know the language.
Then the muscular flanks shining,

a chiseled kind of strength.
The natural aesthetic of the uncut mane.

The sheer beauty of it.
Then putting my foot in the boot

of the narrow stirrup,
I inhaled the fragrance of the leather

before hearing it creak with my weight,
and I settled into the saddle

on the breadth of its massive back.
Before I could even think, the wind

in my hair, the mane flying.
Ride, he said, and I did.

In the timeless instant
before waking again into this life.

GLASS

I heard a bullet-like thud
    before I had gotten out
        of bed, as if someone knocked

on the glass
    porch-side door; but
        it wasn't until later that I heard

the possibly
    window-breaking thud again.
        A sharp-shinned hawk, that must

have seen the reflection
    of herself, or was attempting to
        pick off one of the sparrows that

nest on the north side
    of the porch. I turned—
        the sharp-shinned had returned to

a leafless branch,
    frisking her feathers and
        rotating her head; fluffing herself,

in her attempt to
    brush away the blow of
        her head-first flight into the glass,

and what might have
    appeared to the hawk as an
        opening through the unobstructed

air. There she was: settling;
    twitching; combing her shoulder
        and wing feathers with the curve

of her beak; and to what appeared
    to be mutual surprise, there we were,
        eyeing each other through the glass.

ARIDITY AND THE SPIRITUAL LIFE

It is apparent in the three large terra cotta pots
housing the geraniums on the brick esplanade

around the side of the farmhouse. It is
in the dusty pots resting on black plastic skids

placed above the sand, glittering with mica
on the walk. It is in the dryness which has browned

the grass. It is in such dryness where we can also
flourish, this abeyance between where we might

just lie in the hayed meadow and let the downpour
take us, if there was such abundance.

The dryness is a knowing of the time between
a dry chaffing and more of an arid settling,

an accumulation of dried mud and dust,
the blowing of which distills what is empty in us

so that we become even more barren, abrading
ourselves of our inner tarnish. It is polishing what is

silver within us into the buff of a burnished gleam.
The results of aridity and solitariness are much

like inadvertently soaking up a spilled
drink with one's sleeve. Little things then pique

our gratitude. Sometimes it is only then we hear
the voice of the divine in a donkey's cry.

Part Four

HOVERING MOON

Translations of Federico Garcia Lorca
and Saint John of the Cross

ARBOL DE CANCION

Cana de voz y gesto
una vez y otra vez
tiembla sin esperanza
en el aire de ayer.

La nina suspirando
lo qaueria coger;
ero llegaba siempre
un minute despues.

Ay sol! Ay luna, luna!
un minute despues.
Sesenta flores grises
enredaban sus pies.

Mira como se mece
una y otra vez,
virgin de flor y rama,
en el aire de ayer.

—Federico Garcia Lorca

TREE OF SONG

Reed of voice and gesture
once and again once,
it trembles without hope
in yesterday's air.

The girl sighs, wanting
to catch its essence;
but arrives always
a moment late.

Ay, sun! Ay moon, moon!
a moment late.
Sixty pallid flowers
entangle her feet.

See how she rocks
once and once again—
flower and bough virgin
in yesterday's air.

ADELINA DE PASEO

La mar no tiene naranjas,
ni Sevilla tiene amor.
Morena, que luz de fuego.
Prestame tu quitasol.

Me pondra la cara verde
—zumo de lima y limon—
tus palabras—pececillos--
nadaran alrededor.

La mar no tiene naranjas.
Ay, amor.
Ni Sevilla tiene amor!

   —Federico Garcia Lorca

SONG OF ADELINE, THE STREETWALKER

There are no oranges in the sea,
there's no love in Seville.
Tawny girl, your glances blaze—
share your parasol.

I'll tint my face green
—with the juice of lemons and limes—
your words—just little fish—
finning around.

As far as oranges,
the sea has none—
Oh, love,
neither is there any love in Seville.

CANCION DE JINETE

Cordoba.
Lejana y sola.

Jaca negra, luna grande,
y aceitunas en mi alforja.
Aunque sepa los caminos
yo nunca llegare a Cordoba.

Por el llano, por el viento,
jaca negra, luna roja.
La muerta me esta mirando
desde las torres de Cordoba.

Ay que camino tan largo!
Ay mi jaca valerosa!
Ay, que la muerta me espera,
antes de llegar a Cordoba!

Cordoba!
Lejana y sola.

—Federico Garcia Lorca

SONG OF THE RIDER

Cordoba!
Distant and alone.

Dark pony, large moon,
and a saddlebag of olives.
Although I know these roads,
I may never reach Cordoba.

Over the plain, through the wind,
little black mare, tangerine moon.
Death itself looks about
along the ramparts of Cordoba.

Ah, the long endless road!
Oh, my dark pony's valiant heart!
Ay, that my death should await me
before I arrive in Cordoba!

Cordoba!
So distant and alone.

REFRAN

Marzo
pasa volano.

Y Enero sigue tan alto.

Enero,
sigue en la noche del cielo.

Y abajo Marzo es un momento.

Enero.
Para mis ojos viejos.

Marzo.
Para mis frescas manos.

—Federico Garcia Lorca

PROVERB

March
is flying past.

And January goes
along so high.

January,
streams forth in the night sky.

And below March occurs
in barely a minute.

January,
for my old man's eyes.

March,
for my freezing hands.

BALANZA

La noche quieta siempre.
El dia va y viene.

La noche muerta y alta.
El dia con un ala.

La noche sobre espejos
y el dia bajo el viento.

—Federico Garcia Lorca

BALANCE

Night is quiet—always.
It is day that goes and comes.

Dead of night soaring.
Day with its wing.

Night hovering above mirrors,
And day stirring beneath the wind.

CANCION DEL MARIQUITA

El mariquita se peine
en su peinador de seda.

Los vecinos se sonrien
en sus ventanas posteras.

El mariquita organiza
los bucles de su cabeza.

Por los patios gritan loros,
surtidores de planetas.

El mariquita se adorna
con un jazmin sinverguenza.

La tarde se pone extrana
de peines y enredaderas.

El escandalo temblaba
rayado como una cebra.

Los mariquitas del Sur
cantan en las azoteas!

—Federico Garcia Lorca

SONG OF THE LADYBUG

The ladybug combs her hair
in her gown of silk.

The neighbors smile
through their rear windows.

The ladybug dresses
each curl on her head.

The parrots scream from the patios,
the planets fly by.

The ladybug adorns herself
with a jasmine perfume.

Littering the afternoon
are combs and brushes.

Scandal herself hovers,
striped like a zebra.

The ladybugs from the South
carol from the roofs.

AL ODO DE UNA MUCHACHA

No quise.
No quise decirte nada.

Vi en tus ojos
dos arbolitos locos.
De brisa, de risa y de oro.

Se meneaban.
No quise.

No quise decirte nada.

—Federico Garcia Lorca

CONFIDING IN A GIRL

No, I wouldn't.
No, I wouldn't tell you a thing.

In your eyes, I see
two crazy lithe trees.

They laugh. They smile.
They are golden.

They dazzle.
But she is equivocating . . .

No, I wouldn't.
No, I wouldn't tell you anything.

LA LUNA ASOMA

Cuando sale la luna
se pierden las companas
y aparecen las sendas
impenetrables.

Cuando sale la luna
el mar cubre la tierra
y el corazon se siente
isla en el infinito.

Nadie come naranjas
bajo la luna llena.
Es preciso comer
fruta verde y helada.

Cuando sale la luna
de cien rostros iguales,
la moneda de plata
solloza en el bolsillo.

—Federico Garcia Lorca

HOVERING MOON

When the moon emerges
it loosens the bells
and the paths appear
untraversable.

When the moon emerges
the sea sweeps over the land
and the heart is overtaken—
cut off by what is infinite.

No one devours oranges
beneath the full moon.
No need to ingest
green, frostbitten fruit.

When the moon emerges
with a hundred uniform faces,
so many pieces of silver
sob in their coin purse.

EN UNA NOCHE OSCURA

En una noche oscura,
con ansias, en amores inflamada,
¡oh dichosa ventura!,
salí sin ser notada,
estando ya mi casa sosegada;

a escuras y segura
por la secreta escala, disfrazada,
¡oh dichosa ventura!,
a escuras y encelada,
estando ya mi casa sosegada;

en la noche dichosa,
en secreto, que naide me veía
ni yo miraba cisa,
sin otra luz y guía
sino la que en el corazón ardía.

Aquesta me guiaba
más cierto que la luz del mediodía
adonde me esperaba
quien yo bien me sabía
en parte donde naide parecía.

¡Oh noche que guiaste!
¡oh noche amable más que la alborada!;
¡oh noche que juntaste,
Amado con amada,
amada en el Amado transformada!

En mi pecho florido,
que entero para él solo se guardaba,
allí quedó dormido,
y yo le regalaba,
y el ventalle de cedros aire daba.

El aire del almena,
cuando yo sus cabellos esparcía,
con su mano serena
en mi cuello hería,
y todos mis sentidos suspendía.

Quedéme y olvidéme,
el rostro recliné sobre el Amado;
cesó todo y dejéme,
dejando mi cuidado
entre las azucenas olvidado.

      —St. John of the Cross

DARK NIGHT

In the dark night
lit with desire, inflamed by the fire of love,
(oh, grace of flight)
I am bereft
since being in my house is tranquil.

Secure and dark,
ever higher up a secret ladder, disguised,
(oh, grace of flight)
the darkness became a trap
since being in my house is tranquil.

Without that night of delight,
in secret, without anyone seeing me,
neither my seeking anything,
without a guide or a light,
except for the one lit within my heart.

That light has continued guiding me,
more certain than midday sun
where I could abide by my expectations,
how well I was known there by the One—
where no one else seemed to be.

Oh, night that guided me.
Oh, night more loving than the dawn.
Oh, night that unites
Lover with loved one,
beloved in Lover—transformed!

Upon the flowering of my heart,
I guarded it completely for the One
taking comfort there,
and I was grateful I could offer Him
the fragrant winds fanning through the cedars.

Gusts swirled at the parapet,
just where one's hair is blown about—
and by His hand's serene touch,
he intentionally wounded my neck—
when all of my senses became suspended.

Remaining, I lost my being,
my face rested upon my Lover there—
everything ceased, freeing me,
leaving all my cares
abandoned among the forgotten lilies.

SUMA DE PERFECCIÓN

Olvido de lo criado,
memoria del Criador,
atencion a lo interior
y estarse amando al Amado.

—St. John of the Cross

SUM OF PERFECTION

To ignore the created and inferior,
to always remember the creator,
to give full attention to the interior,
and to be open to love the Beloved Lover.

Part Five

MNEMOSYNE:
A SUITE FOR THE MUSES

EUTERPE SINGING

(Euterpe: Music)

Sing for me, I said, and she did.
She sang such simple lyrics

to what goes beyond language.
Teach me, I said,

and she answered, *I will
show you swinging ropes of song,*

*but you will be able to hold
nothing,* and her voice rose.

Show me, I said, *how
to sing,* and placed my hands

together in prayer.
Sing for me, she said, and I did.

ACCOMPANIMENT

(Clio: History)

Not unlike the yellow birch leaf
we saw suspended above the edge

of the trail by a thread of a spider's web
in autumn rain on Mount Toby, what remains

of us in the warmth of spring sunlight
in a meadow in Conway is still held

in abeyance above bedstraw and meadow grass.
I have thought of you often this morning.

You don't know this. And you don't need me
to tell you, but I need you to know that

you accompany me into the world
like a rose opening.

KINGDOM OF HEAVEN

(*Polyhmnia: Hymns*)

The father's kingdom is spread out upon the earth and
people do not see it.
  —The Gospel of Thomas

After judging each wreath
hung on every door on Beacon Hill

on a scale of one to five stars,
we sit facing each other Christmas evening

in the bedroom in your Aunt Striddie's
Empire chairs. Streetlights illumine

the blizzard's gusts that shine
over the snow angels we made—

the candles blown out in the igloo
of snowballs we built to house them in.

You ask me: *How does this begin?*
and *Why don't other people want this?*

Beneath the lamplight, I draw breath,
the freckles on your Scandinavian face

only even more abundant on the long
fingers of your elegant hands. I say:

It starts with the meeting of our eyes,
and *Too often it is what people do not see.*

WHAT IS FAMILIAR

(Thalia: Comedy)

is how I massage those ropes
of tightened muscles across

your shoulders and upper back,
placing my hands beneath the top

of your blouse, while I stand
behind you beside the kitchen sink,

so I may be able to work
what is tender loose.

I read your skin as I would a map,
my fingers adept at locating the pain

there with the pressure of my touch.
You ask me, *Do you hear it pop?*

and then I feel your release.
What is familiar are the kisses

I place on your bare shoulders,
grateful for the gift

of those moments, before we spend
the remainder of the afternoon

bundling magazines with string
for the Salvation Army,

you placing your index finger
on each knot I am about to tie.

WABI AND SABI

(Terpsichore: Dance)

We rub our hands over the bench along the trail
to feel what weather has worn,

how storms have polished the pine wood—
she flows inside of me like a spring.

Other times, she becomes the wind
in the trees, the trailing voices of geese.

On those mornings, I watch the light
rise in her to rekindle her face—

the way she looked, that Sunday, across
the wildflower meadow at Northwest Park:

Deptford pink, black-eyed Susan,
the open white parasols of Queen Anne's lace.

I know when I become as obdurate as stone,
the Christ in me breaks the stone in two,

and I become a fountain
pouring out of the cleaved rock.

THE INSPIRED LIFE

(Melpomeme, Originally "The Muse of the Chorus")

Angels speak homeopathy fluently.
   —Caroline Myss

The fingers of my hands find
a way to her the other evening,

working out the kink in the right side
of her neck, and when the muscles

finally relax, she releases
one audible sigh, *Oh.*

Blue morning glories spiral above
white trillium, their petals opened

beneath their diamond-shaped leaves.
The wood pewee calls out above us

among the trellises in the garden,
and the one this morning answers

from her perch over the trail above me;
the pattern of a shepherd's crook

uncurling in every fiddlehead
that rises through the ground.

HUMMINGBIRD AND STAR

(Urania: Astronomy)

Whether we sit hip to hip on a boulder
in the middle of Roaring Brook—

our feet cooling in the rush;
or whether we picnic in a hayed meadow

looking up at summer sky.
That simplicity is what we

try to live out of. Promise me
you will remember the hummingbird

pollinating those blue
irises purpling the banks of the reservoir—

what we find in each other's face
that radiates like the light of a star.

RITUALS

(*Erato: Lyric Poetry*)

At twilight, I walk the land I cleared
of brier, pigweed, and nettle,

turn to look through the kitchen
window on the side of the cabin,

know the warmth there inside
by the lights I turned on.

There are mornings I watch dawn
fill the grove of pine and hickory,

see stars in the cup of the dipper
through treetops, hear an owl hoot,

as it changes its perch from one limb
to another in the woods

on the ridge across Market Hill Road.
But at twilight I find stillness in the falling

of pine needles, how they spread out
over open ground, and it is in stillness,

I remember how I brush back her hair,
take her face in my hands, so I can see

what shines there, the way sudden wind
lifts branches to allow a slant of light

to make yellow hickory leaves more yellow
and its green leaves more green.

MNEMOSYNE

(Goddess of Memory & the Muses)

They are happy, they are just beginning. They sit and talk
about their need for simplicity, and the tension between them

grows, the way iron filaments are drawn by a magnet.
Before he kisses her, he notices the curves of her breasts

beneath the black crinoline dress; then how everything
ceases except the touch of what is sensual.

He looks at her face in the sun, the small blue veins that etch
her closed eyelids, after he opens his, the beads of sweat above

her lips. This is the beginning of their learning what is sublime:
how they stand on East Beach, and look over at Block Island;

how they watch the green sea spread out at low tide,
the surf entreating them with the *adagio*

of what is susurrant; how they hold each other against the wind
that doesn't appear to ripple the water.

THE FIRE

(Epyllion: "Little Epic")

He gathers cordwood into his arms,
lays each piece on the grates

in the hearth, two across and two over;
sets balled newsprint with a match,

and the wood and paper blaze up
in a *whoosh* of brightness.

He first watches the blue flames,
then the white, those lights they see

when they are together,
the incandescent tongues that burst

above his head when he speaks to her
about what they share is sacred.

He considers what light and warmth are,
that the glow of the fire doesn't compare

to what shines in her face, that rose
beneath the surface of her skin.

When he banks up burning embers
with the long-handled shovel, then uses

the iron tongs to gather the fallen
ingots of wood back onto the grates,

he leans into the fire, and hears her voice
when he was above her, praying for her

silently, with her hands on his back,
how she told him, *I can feel the heat.*

A DREAM LIKE OURS

(Kore/Persephone, Rebirth)

I must tell you
what your words do—

how they fill me.
May you infuse the distance

between us in such a way.
May what I feel for you

immerse you, always; in this
dream that is ours,

from which, if I ever do
awaken, may it be looking

into your face, whose
depths are inherent with

such intrigue they reveal
themselves with

mystique, so that I am
always surprised, due to

my disbelief, that it is you
who are the one here

with me; it is you
I see when I open my eyes.

Part Six

SIXTEEN TRANSLATIONS FROM THE ITALIAN OF GIUSEPPE UNGARETTI

Sentimento del Tempo (Sentiment of Time), 1919-1935;
Il Dolore (Grief), 1937-1946; and *Ultimi Cori Per La Terra Promessa*
(Last Choruses for the Promised Land), Rome, 1952-1960

SILENZIO IN LIGURIA

1922

from Sentimento del Tempo, 1919–1935

Scade flessuosa la pianura d'acqua.

Nelle sue urne il sole
Ancora segreto si bagna.

Una carnagione lieve transcorre.

Ed ella apre improvvisa ai seni
La grande mitezza degli occhi.

L'ombra sommersa delle rocce muore.

Dolce sbocciata delle anche ilari,
Il vero amore e una quiete accesa,

E la godo diffua
Dall'ala alabastrina
D'una mattina immobile.

SILENCE IN LIGURIA

1922

from Sentiment of Time, 1919–1935

The supple plain of water dries up.

In its urns the sun
bathes, still a secret.

A delicate complexion slips by.

And in her suddenly revealing her breasts
The immense tenderness of her eyes gleam.

The submerged shadow of the rocks fades.

Sweet blossomed from lithe hips,
True love is a luminous stillness,

And I take delight in it
From an alabaster wing
On a motionless morning.

OGNI GRIGIO

1925

from Sentimento del Tempo, 1919–1935

Dalla spoglie di serpe
Alla pavida talpa
Ogni grigio si gingilla sui duomi . . .

Come una prora bionda
Di Stella in stella il sole s'accomiata
E s'acciglia sotto la pergola . . .

Come una fronte stanca
E riapparsa la notte
Nel cavo d'una mano . . .

EACH GRAY

1925

from Sentiment of Time, 1919–1935

From molting snake
To frightened mole
Every gray plays on the domed cathedral . . .

Like a blonde bow
From star to star the sun departs
And glowers beneath the arbor . . .

Like a tired brow,
Night reappears
In the hollow of one's hand . . .

CON FUCCO

1925

from Sentimento del Tempo, 1919–1935

Con fucco d'occhi un nostalgico lupo
Scorre la quiete nuda.

Non trova che ombre di cielo sul ghiaccio,

Fondono serpi fatue e brevi viole.

WITH FIRE

1925

from Sentiment of Time, 1919–1935

With the fiery eyes of a homesick wolf
scans the naked quiet.

He finds only shadows of the sky on the ice,

Blending conspicuous snakes and evanescent violets.

ULTIMO QUARTO

1927

from Sentimento del Tempo, 1919–1935

Luna,
Piuma di cielo,
Cosi velina,
Arida,
Transporti il murmure d'anime spoglie?

E all pallid che diranno mai
Pipistrelli dai ruderi del teatro,
In sogno quelle capre,
E fra arse foglie come in fermo fumo
Con tutto il suo sgolarsi di cristallo
Un usignuolo?

LAST QUARTER

1927

from Sentiment of Time, 1919–1935

Moon,
Sky feather,
Soft tissue,
Deserted,
Do you carry the murmuring of naked souls?

And all pale will they never speak of
Bats from the ruins of the theater,
Those goats in a dream,
And in the overhanging smoke of smoldering leaves
With all of its crystalline singing
A nightingale?

STATUA

1927

from Sentimento del Tempo, 1919–1925

Gioventu impietrita,
O statua, o staua dell'abisso umano . . .

Il gran tumulto dopo tanto viaggio
Corrode uno scoglio
A fiore di labbra.

STATUE

1927

from *Sentiment of Time, 1919–1925*

Petrified youth,
O statue, o statue of the human abyss . . .

After the long journey the great tumult
Corrodes a stone
That flowers from its lips.

STELLE

from Sentimento del Tempo, 1919–1935

Tornano in alto ad ardere le favole.

Cadranno colle foglie al primo vento.

Ma venga un altro soffio,
Ritornera scintillamento nuovo.

STARS

from Sentiment of Time, 1919–1935

The myths are back up on high.

At the first wind, they will fall with the leaves.

But with just another breath,
Sparkling will return anew.

GRIDO

1928

from Sentimento del Tempo, 1919–1935

Giunta la sera,
Riposavo sopra l'erba monotona,
E presi gusto
A quella brama senza fine,
Grido torbido e alato
Che la luce quando muore trattiene.

OUTBURST

1928

from Sentiment of Time, 1919–1935

Evening has come,
resting on the monotonous grass,
I cherish
The perpetual ache,
The turbid, winged outburst
That the light holds when it dies.

QUIETE

1929

from Sentimento del Tempo, 1919–1935

L'uva e matura, il camp arato,

Si stacca il monte dalle nuvole.

Sui polverosi specchi dell'estate
Caduta e l'ombra,

Tra le dita incerte
Il loro lume e chiaro,
E lontano.

Colle rondini fugge
L'ultimo strazio.

QUIET

1929

from Sentiment of Time, 1919–1935

The grapes mellow and the field's plowed,

The mountain detaches from the clouds.

On the dusty mirrors of summer
Shadows fall,

Between uncertain fingers
their light is clear,
and it is distant

With the swallows fleeing
The ultimate torment

DOVE LA LUCE

1930

from Sentimento del Tempo, 1919–1935

Come allodole ondosa
Nel vento lieto sui giovanni prati,
Le braccia ti sanno leggero, vieni.

Ci scorderemo di quaggiu,
E del male e del cielo,
E del mio sangue rapido alla Guerra,
Di passi d'ombre memori
entro rossori di mattina nuove.

Dove non muove foglie piu la luce,
Sogni e crucci passato ad altre rive,
Dov'e posata sera,
Vienti ti porter
Alle colline d'oro.

L'ora costante, liberi d'eta,
Nel suo perduto nimbo
Sara nostro lenzuolo.

WHERE THE LIGHT

1930

from Sentiment of Time, 1919–1935

Like the wavy flight of larks
On the delightful wind over new meadows,
Come, my arms will begin to know your weightlessness.

We'll forget about all that's down here,
And of both evil and of heaven,
And my blood quickening to war,
And the tracked shadows in memory
By a new red dawn.

Where the light no longer moves the leaves,
Dreams and worries pass to other shores,
Where there is evening,
Come, I'll carry you
To the golden hills.

The constant hour, free of age,
Its lost halo
Will be our sheet.

SERA

from Sentimento del Tempo, 1919–1935

Appie dei passi della sera
Va u'acqua chiara
Colore l'ulivo,

E giunge al breve fuoco smemorato.

Nel fumo ora odo grilli e rane,

Dove tenere tremano erbe.

WHAT WILL BE

from Sentiment of Time, 1919–1935

At the steps of evening's passing
Clear water flows
The color of olives,

And it coalesces into a brief forgetful fire.

In the smoke, I hear the crickets and frogs,

Where the herbs and grasses continue to rustle.

CANTO

1932

from Sentimento del Tempo, 1919–1935

Rivedo la tua bocca lenta
(Il mare le va incontra delle notti)
E la cavalla delle reni
In Agonia caderti
Nelle mie braccia che cantavano,
E riportarti un sonno
Al colorito e a nuove morti.

E la crudele solitudine
Che in se ciascuno scopre, se ama,
Ora toma infinita,
Da te mi divide per sempre.

Cara lontana come in uno sprecchio.

SONG

1932

from Sentiment of Time, 1919–1935

I see your deliberate mouth
(Nights the sea rises to meet it)
And the mare of the loins
Thrusts you into agony
In my singing arms,
And lulls you to sleep
Back to color and new deaths.

Now there is an infinite tomb
Dividing me from you always.

We are far away as in a mirror . . .

SILENZIO STELLATO

1932

from Sentimento del Tempo, 1919–1935

E gli alberi e la notte
non si muovono piu
Se non da nidi.

STARRY NIGHT

1932

from Sentiment of Time, 1919–1935

And the trees and the night
have ceased to move at all
Except from their nests.

IL TEMPO E MUTO

from Il Dolore, 1937–1946

Il tempo e muto fra canneti immoti . . .

Lungi d'approdi errava una canoa . . .
Stremato, inerte il rematore . . . I cieli
Gia decaduti a baratri di fumi . . .

Proteso invano all'orla dei ricordi,
Cadere forse fu merce . . .

Non seppe

Ch'e la stressa illusion mondo e mente,
Che nel mister delle proprie onde
Ogni terrena voce fa naufragio.

TIME IS SILENT

from Grief, 1937–1946

Time is silent among the motionless reeds . . .

A canoe drifted far from shore . . .
The rower exhausted, inert . . . The skies
Already decayed into smoky abysses . . .

Stretched in vain to the edge of memories,
Falling was perhaps a thing unto itself . . .

        He did not know

That is the illusion of the world and the mind,
That in the tension of its own waves
Every earthly voice is shipwrecked

L'ANGELO DEL POVARO

from Il Dolore, 1937–1946

Ora che invade le oscurate menti
Piu aspra pieta del sangue e della terra,
Ora che ci misura ad ogni palpito
Il silenzio di tante inguiuste morti,

Ora si svegli l'angelo del povero,
Gentilezza superstite dell'anima . . .

Col gesto inestinguibile dei secoli
Discenda a capo del suo vecchio popolo,
In mezzo alle ombre . . .

THE ANGEL OF THE POOR

from Grief, 1937–1946

Now that it invades the darkened minds
More bitter pity than blood and earth,
Now that it treasures us within every heartbeat
The silence of so many innocent dead.

Now the angel of the poor awakens,
The soul's surviving kindnesses . . .

With the inextinguishable gesture of the centuries
May it descend to lead its ancient people,
Amidst the shadows . . .

VARIAZIONI SU NULLA

from Il Dolore, 1937–1946

Quel nonnulla di sabbía che transcorre
Dalla clessidra muto e va posandosi,
E, fugaci, le impronte sul carnato,
Sul carnato che muore, d'una nube . . .

Poi mano che rovescia la clessidra,
Il ritorno per muoversi, di sabía,
Il farsi argentea tacito di nube
Ai primi brevi lividi dell'alba . . .

La mano in ombra la clessidra volse,
E, di sabbía, il nonnulla che transcorre
Silente, e unica cosa che ormai s'oda
E, essendo udita, in buio non scompiaia.

VARIATIONS ON NOTHING

from Grief, 1937–1946

That trifle of sand that passes
Out of the silent hourglass and settles down,
And, transitory, the notion of the flesh,
On the flesh that perishes, of a cloud . . .

Then the hand overturns the hourglass,
Returning the flow to the reflowing, of sand,
The silent silvery making of a cloud
At the first brief streaks of dawn . . .

The hand in the shadow turns the hourglass,
And, of sand, the trifle passes
Silently, and the only thing that is now known
And, being heard, does not vanish in the dark

PER SEMPRE

Roma, il 24 Maggio 1959

from Ultimi Cori Per La Terra Promessa, Roma, 1952–1960

Senza niuna impazienza songnero,
Mi pieghero al lavoro
Che non puo mai finire,
E a poco a poca in cima
Alle braccia rinate
Si reapriranno mani soccorrevoli,
Nella cavita loro
Riapparsi gli occhi, ridaranno luce,
E, de'iomprovviso intatta
Sarai risorta, mi fara da guida
Di nuovo la tua voce,
Per sempre ti rivedo.

FOREVER

Rome, 24 May 1959

from Last Choruses from the Promised Land, 1952–1960

Without any impatience I dream,
I will bend to the labor
That can never cease.
And little by little at the ends
Of rejuvenated arms,
Helping hands will open again,
In their cavity
Reappearing eyes return light,
And, suddenly, intact
You will resurrect to guide me
Again with your voice,
I will see you forever.

Part Seven

SHARING STORIES AT LUNCH

SACRAMENTAL ACTS

It was the yellow mixing bowl
my mother handed down to me
when I was a child
when she was making her homemade
apple pie. It was the tastes

from that bowl I remember—
the tang of cinnamon and nutmeg
licked from a finger
that swirled immemorial sweetness
on the tongue, blended

with delectable bits of sliced apples.
It was the small can
of hot dogs and beans my mother
warmed by holding it with tongs
and a hot pad over a candle

when we lost power
during hurricanes in Miami.
Those unappetizing bite-sized
wieners never tasted so good.
But I was never more comforted

any more than that
in all of my childhood by being
blanketed in the warmth
of my mother in that glow,
the rain pelting the windows.

It was those pies my mother made
out of King Arthur flour and Crisco,
especially the banana cream
and the lemon meringue—
always luscious and tart,

light and sweet, topped with
towers of cream and meringue;
when each piece was sliced,
they shook, as did the pie itself,
when they were passed from counter

to table, or from pie dish to plate.
It was the borscht my father made
every Easter, thick with beets,
that would fill the air with an earthy
fragrance of nourishment, which

he would add a sliced hardboiled egg
into his bowl that was spiked with
a dollop of sour cream. It was
also the chuck and pork he would
grind up fresh in the meat grinder,

then stuff that into the casings
he bought along with handfuls
of chopped garlic that would be
baked to compliment the miracle
of the Easter meal, always concluding

with a taste of the raw honey from
my Polish uncle's hive, always begun
with the passing of the communion
wafer, making us feel preternaturally
blessed as the host melted

in the mouth. It is the meals I prepare
in our small kitchen that we share
all that we eat and drink over
the oblong sewing table we use
for breakfast, lunch, and dinner—

whether it is blueberry scones,
tuna fish on toasted cinnamon-raisin
English muffins, stuffed salmon,
pesto chicken rolled in panko
breadcrumbs, cauliflower soup

with sweet red peppers and chives,
or homemade pasta Bolognese,
it is the succulence of what we eat
that informs our lives by each bite
we take, each spoonful we savor,

and every sip of red wine
that washes over our tongue.
By these sacramental acts we toast
our health, the moment, the day
in laying down each memory.

RED-BELLIED WOODPECKER

Red-bellied is counterintuitive,
    since your head is streaked
        with a band of crimson,

which I first saw rounding
    the trunk of the shagbark
        while I stood still as a stone

amid the coolness and dew,
    looking at the summer
        horizon, morning cumulous

blowing through the sky.
    Your low guttural annoyance
        upon seeing me ceased, since

you were able to sense
    I would do no harm—
        still as I was, and distant

by a few steps
    so I could study you:
        claws scratching the upturned

cantilevered sections of bark,
    wearing your crosshatch
        black and white back feathers

like a camouflage tuxedo, beak
    darting between each bark
        layer until you seized the prize—

a long earwig within
    a crevice, squirming at the tip
        of your nib, but lodged there

firmly, before adjusting
    yourself, and, leaping, in a start,
        up into flight with fare for your

chicks. How you have
    completed me by hitching
        around the shagbark trunk

in your woodsy ways; how
    upon take-off, I undulate
        with you, winging through air.

GREEN HERON, FIRST DAY OF AUTUMN

We don't see you
    at first passing the pond but
        we notice you striding back—

blending in with the branches
    of deadfall pointing to the sky.
        You embody stillness,

your reflection ripples in
    the water's surface, the sere
        wind simmering through

the willows. Its sibilance
    a counterpoint to your vigilant
        quietude. We take a few steps

closer and you turn your head—
    its green luminescence gleaming
        in the afternoon sunlight. But

then you turn back to your work
    that is not work but your nature,
        to whatever it is that has caught

your attention, and without a splash
    your head breaks toward the pond,
        penetrating its surface with your

beak, swinging your body as does
    a trapeze artist, claws clutching
        the branch, peach-yellow abdomen

brandished momentarily,
    in your lunging toward fish or frog,
        and then draw yourself back up

again to rest in your hunkered fishing
    posture, as a monk or nun at prayer,
        cloistered within your inner silence.

We are nourished by your calm,
    bolstered by your practiced acrobatics,
        your return to your pond meditations.

The wind picks up toward evening—
    a chill descending, the clouds tinted rouge.
        You stay, but we must go.

LINGERING BESIDE LONG POND, INDIAN SUMMER

Sitting beneath the river birch,
yellow leaves parsed
and falling in the wind,

we watch
a pale green scarf that rises
then floats over the blue pond,

as it lands
fluttering over the ripples,
pulling in its wings

to set down its stick legs
in the cool gray mud,
to unveil its true form,

after masquerading
as anything but itself—
this magician, this master angler,

standing in silence
amid the willows,
and wading among the reeds,

where the heron takes comfort
beside the floating deadwood
to become invisible again.

BROAD-WINGED

Looking up upon first sighting,
I heard the word *buteo*,

in my mind, uncannily floating
with an agility such as yours,

as you hovered, spiraled,
and displayed above us

on our walk beneath
a cloudless December afternoon.

Buteo, is your scientific name,
your classification, but what

makes you specific is its appendage,
platypterus, more commonly known

as broad-winged hawk, a bird of prey
known for soaring, as you so aptly do,

riding ripples of wind
the way the blind read Braille,

feeling your way with such
a tensile touch and strength that

you reveal each air current itself,
and while exposing it, you become

its illustrator of the invisible,
your call keying your mate, whom

we hadn't seen, until you steeply dove
down to the ground to the scrub ditch

to hunt behind the pines,
and rose again, to meet her cries,

the two of you circling above us
in a contented airborne choreography

that nearly stalls as you turn, suspended,
where you both float momentarily

in stillness, not inert, but active,
invoking a trance, a meditation,

the beneficence of rapture
in observing the plump bodies

and stout wings of raptors coursing, then
pausing to etch their flight in the air.

MINIATURE CAMERA

a gift for Tevis Kimball & Marsha Peters

It's Lilliputian lens
opens wide as does an archive of memory
of one refined image
after another of the many

memorable times of those years
in Providence: the arty lofts
and stylish restaurants, with potbellied
stoves, that still warm us;

those casual Newport tea rooms
and plush seaside inns,
whose names we may have
misplaced, but whose set of keys

felicitously open any mnemonic door
we would have entered together,
whose sunny dispositions
continue to grace the hallways

of reminiscence with echoes, and whose
bright reflections of the design
of Art Deco tiles perpetuate
and consistently pique me into savor

of not only who we were
but who we are, soaring
as that red-tailed hawk
hovering over the campus pond,

morning light filtering
through that rouged band of feathers,
all those years of friendship
spanning more than a half century

caught in the shutter click
of a single instant, which appears
to only clarify, as does the hawk's image
rising to the zenith of the day moon.

SWEET RED PEPPERS

for Michael Miller

To see you in your element
selecting the most superior
sweet red peppers from
the wooden basket on the top
shelf of the produce section,
sizing them up for how
they might fit into your
sauté pan, if they may have

any imperfections, possibly
choosing the darker colored
reds for their sweetness,
their poignance, spreading
over the palate, combined
with the fried tempeh that
you would brown afterwards
in olive oil and a little butter

in the same pan to more fully
absorb the dulcet taste
of sweet red peppers, I could
only imagine is the same way
you choose your metaphors
and similes, and those exacting
images you so thoughtfully
layer throughout your poems,

whose craft is not only sound
but often as impeccable in
their marriage of aesthetics
and utility so as to create
a made thing that perpetuates
beyond its initial ideation,
when after draft after draft
the work itself reaches a polish,

whose shine resembles
those windows of light found
reflected on the skins
of the sweet red peppers that
you place from their basket
on the shelf into your carriage,
your mouth breaking into
a smile, which reveals what

can be realized in what is life-
affirming, in taking satisfaction
in discerning quality, as to which
are the best vegetables to select
at the market, and what may
make a poem as memorable as
a sandwich of sautéed tempeh
and the choicest sweet red peppers.

SHARING STORIES AT LUNCH

You finish your milk
and lift your tumbler so you can look
out of the clear glass bottom
at me, while scrunching up
your nose and mouth to make a face
as we become two elders at play
reliving our childhoods.

I recount how I requested
an extra half glass of milk
so that I could stay up later
with the adults, or watch that extra
fifteen minutes of television,
coaxing the contents of my glass
into lasting long past

the allotted time my mother
would normally allow,
especially since I would tell her
that the milk at the bottom
of the glass was like the moon
setting; the more I drank the more
the moon would disappear,

and since I didn't want the moon
to vanish, I wanted to savor
the remaining sips of milk,
of which mother replied
that she thought I might become
a writer when I was a man,
which was something I had forgotten

from childhood. Then you recalled
your own memory as a girl,
when Marilyn MacCabbie, your best
friend, and you would be ushered
into the family car by her father,
with the rest of the family during
a thunderstorm, since they lived in

an old farmhouse, because he was
petrified of lightning striking any
of the children. You would all sit
in the parked car in the safety of
the garage until the storm had passed.
And upon hearing your story, I felt
a similar warmth upon imagining you

safe after weathering the storm, and came to
appreciate the camaraderie of the moment.
Then I lifted my own emptied glass,
and looked at you out of the clear
bottom of the tumbler, and smiled at you
smiling across from me—
fortified by our having shared stories

over lunch, lingering a few moments
longer, held somewhere between
the haven of Marilyn MacCabbie's
father's garage during a thunderstorm
and my nursing my pastel aluminum
cup, where we both could finish our milk
and watch the moon set before it vanished.

AUTHOR'S NOTE

 WALLY SWIST is the author of over forty books and chapbooks of poetry and prose.

Among his books are *The Daodejing: A New Interpretation*, with co-authors, David Breeden and Steven Schroeder (Beaumont, TX: Lamar University Press, 2015). His book *Huang Po and the Dimensions of Love* was selected as the co-winner of the 2011 Crab Orchard Series Open Poetry Contest, judged by Pulitzer Prize-winning poet Yusef Komunyakaa; the book was published by Southern Illinois University Press in 2012, and was nominated for a National Book Award.

Swist is the winner of the 2018 Ex Ophidia Press Poetry Prize for *A Bird Who Seems to Know Me: Poems and Haiku Regarding Birds & Nature*. The book was published in late 2019 by master printer and book designer Gabriel Rummonds, of Bainbridge Island, Washington. He has also published five previous books of poetry with Shanti Arts, of Brusnwick, Maine, including *Candling the Eggs* (2016), *The Map of Eternity* (2018), *The Bees of the Invisible* (2019), *Evanescence: Selected Poems* (2020), and *Awakening & Visitation* (2020) .

His books of nonfiction include *Singing for Nothing: Selected Nonfiction as Literary Memoir* (Brooklyn, NY: The Operating System, 2018), *On Beauty: Essays, Reviews, Fiction, and Plays* (New York & Lisbon: Adelaide Books, 2018), and *A Writer's Statements on Beauty: New and Selected Essays and Reviews* (Brunswick, Maine: Shanti Arts, 2021).

Some of Swist's work has been set to music. This includes his poem "The Rush of the Brook Stills the Mind," which inspired a composition by the electroacoustic composer Dr. Elainie Lillios. The composition was performed by percussionist Scott Deal in Jordan Hall at the New England Conservatory of Music in Boston, Massachusetts, on June 20, 2013. It is only one of several venues across the country where the composition has been performed. Dr. Elainie Lillios is Professor of Composition at Bowling Green State University.

His poem "After Long Drought" was also composed to an electroacoustical score written by Professor Lillios, and the composition was also premiered at Jordan Hall at the New England Conservatory of Music, in June 2016 by percussionist Scott Deal.

A recipient of Artist's Fellowships in poetry from the Connecticut Commission on the Arts (1977 and 2003), Swist was also awarded a one-year writing residency (1998) and two back-to-back one-year writing residencies (2003–2005) at Fort Juniper, the Robert Francis Homestead, in Cushman, Massachusetts, the home of his former mentor.

Swist's poetry and prose have appeared in such national periodicals as *Buddhist Poetry Review, Chiron Review, Commonweal, Ezra: An Online Journal of Translation, The North American Review, Pensive: A Global Journal of Spirituality and the Arts, Rattle, Rolling Stone, Today's American Catholic, Transference: A Literary Journal Featuring the Art & Process of Translation, The Woven Tale Press: The Web's Premier Online Literary and Fine Art Magazine, Your Impossible Voice,* and *Yankee Magazine.*

He currently makes his home in New England, where he continues to write and translate. Although he is semi-retired, he works as a freelance editor, writer, and researcher.

SHANTI ARTS

NATURE ▪ ART ▪ SPIRIT

Please visit us online
to browse our entire book catalog,
including poetry collections and fiction,
books on travel, nature, healing, art,
photography, and more.

Also take a look at our highly
regarded art and literary journal,
Still Point Arts Quarterly, which
may be downloaded for free.

www.shantiarts.com